PARROTS

TROPICAL AND RAINFOREST BIRDS

Tom Jackson

Consultant: Michael Chinery

LORENZ BOOKS

C O N

This edition is published by Lorenz Books

Lorenz Books is an imprint of
Anness Publishing Ltd
Hermes House 88–89 Blackfriars Road, London
SE1 8HA tel. 020 7401 2077; fax 020 7633 9499
www.lorenzbooks.com; info@anness.com

© Anness Publishing Ltd 2004

UK agent: The Manning Partnership Ltd,
6 The Old Dairy, Melcombe Road, Bath BA2
3LR; tel. 01225 478444; fax 01225 478440;
sales@manning-partnership.co.uk

UK distributor: Grantham Book Services Ltd,
Isaac Newton Way, Alma Park Industrial Estate,
Grantham, Lincs NG31 9SD; tel. 01476 541080;
fax 01476 541061; orders@gbs.tbs-ltd.co.uk

North American agent/distributor: National
Book Network, 4501 Forbes Boulevard, Suite
200, Lanham, MD 20706; tel. 301 459 3366;
fax 301 429 5746; www.nbnbooks.com

Australian agent/distributor: Pan Macmillan
Australia, Level 18, St Martins Tower, 31 Market
St, Sydney, NSW 2000; tel. 1300 135113; fax 1300
135103; customer.service@macmillan.com.au

New Zealand agent/distributor: David Bateman
Ltd, 30 Tarndale Grove, Off Bush Road, Albany,
Auckland; tel. (09) 415 7664; fax (09) 415 8892

A CIP catalogue record for this book is
available from the British Library.

Publisher: Joanna Lorenz
Editorial Director: Helen Sudell
Editor: Joy Wotton
Copy Editor: Sarah Brown
Designer: Sarah Williams
Picture Researcher: Cathy Stastny
Illustrators: Martin Knowledon,
    Vanessa Card
Production Controller: Claire Rae

10 9 8 7 6 5 4 3 2 1

T E N T S

What are Tropical Birds?

More birds live in the tropics than anywhere else on Earth. The tropics are the warm regions that lie north and south of the equator. The equator is the imaginary line that divides the planet into the northern hemisphere and the southern hemisphere. The tropics include some of the hottest places on earth as well as some of the wettest and driest. In some places it rains every day, and lush jungles or rainforests grow there. Other areas receive no rain for months on end and are covered by searingly hot, dry deserts. Tropical birds include many different species, from tiny hummingbirds to giant ostriches. They have all evolved in many extraordinary ways to survive in these habitats.

▲ **LUSH JUNGLE**

A blue and yellow macaw flies through a rainforest in South America. Rainforests contain more living things than any other habitat in the world. The plants grow very thickly because of the combination of the high temperatures and the amount of rain that falls. Forest birds, such as this macaw and many other parrots, live alongside all sorts of forest animals.

◄ **WET AND WILD**

An African flock of red-winged pratincoles takes off from a wetland in the Okavango Delta, in Botswana. Tropical wetlands are a magnet for many birds. Some birds spend all year wading through the shallows, searching for food, while other wetland birds choose to migrate from colder places far away, to avoid the cold winter back home.

DRY LAND ▶

Many parts of the tropics are dry and receive very little rain. In some of the drier areas, open grasslands or savannahs form. Water is scarce in these dry grasslands, so all animals, birds and reptiles must gather at the water holes to drink their fill. Grasslands are well known for their large herds of animals, such as antelopes and elephants, but many birds live here, too.

◀ IN THE CLOUDS

Tropical forests that grow high up the sides of mountains are often shrouded in mist. These habitats are called cloudforests. Because the forests are so high up and often gloomy, the bird life that lives there is rarely seen. However, many of the most stunning tropical birds, such as the bird of paradise with its marvellous tail and the resplendent quetzal, make their homes in these remote regions.

GOOD NEIGHBOURS ▶

Because they live in such a crowded place, many tropical animals have had to learn how to get along with other animals and birds. These cattle egrets often hitch a ride on the backs of buffaloes. They feast on the many biting insects that also accompany the buffalo herds.

Focus on the

GREAT GALAH

A flock of galahs perched on a tree in Australia. Galahs are the most common of the cockatoos, most of which live in Australia. Galah cockatoos are generally seen in large flocks as they search for food in dry farmland.

Most of the 350 species of parrot live in the tropics, often in large noisy groups. The parrots are divided into several smaller groups. The larger group of parrots are called macaws, while the smaller parrots are grouped together as parakeets. The other main group of parrots are the cockatoos – large birds that sport a feathered crest on their head. Parrots use their sharp beak to crack nuts and the hard husks of seeds and to scrape out food from larger fruits.

CRESTED PARROT

This sulphur-crested cockatoo has a striking crest on its head and is typical of most of the 18 species of cockatoo. Like all parrots, it has strong grasping feet, ideal for climbing through trees to pluck fruits and nuts from branches.

LITTLE PARROTS

Budgerigars are parrots, or parakeets, to be more precise. This pair is nesting in the Australian outback, where large flocks of budgies travel great distances in search of food and water. Budgies are the most popular pet bird of all, and millions are kept around the world. While wild birds have green and yellow feathers, captive birds have been bred to grow a variety of colourful plumages.

Parrot Family

COLD CLIMATE BIRD

Not all parrots live in the tropics. The kea lives in the mountains of New Zealand. It scavenges for food on the ground, a little like crows do elsewhere, with its unusual pointed bill. This parrot's plumage is much duller than most so it does not stand out while feeding in the open.

POLLEN EATERS

The colourful rainbow lorikeet is a particularly spectacular bird, which lives in Australia and also on many tropical islands. Rainbow lorikeets have a feathery tongue that they use to lick up nectar and pollen from large flowers. They also eat insects. They are conspicuous, noisy birds with bold natures. Like parakeets, lorikeets have more pointed tail feathers than many other, larger, parrots such as macaws and cockatoos, which tend to have blunt, rounded tails.

LARGE AND LONG

This pair of hyacinth macaws lives in the moist forests of South America. They are called hyacinth macaws after their stunning blue feathers, and are among the world's largest parrots, measuring nearly 1m from head to tail tip. They have a blunt, rounded tail and use their mighty bill to crush palm nuts for food. They have a large brain and are thought to be highly intelligent birds.

Rainforest Birds

Tropical rainforests grow in Africa, India, South-east Asia, northern Australasia and South America. Rainforests are very wet. The Amazon Basin, in South America, receives enough rain to fill two billion Olympic swimming pools in just one year! All this rainwater comes from storm clouds that form over the oceans near the equator. With so much rain, the tropical forests grow very quickly and thickly and provide plenty of opportunities for birds to make a living. Parrots, toucans and other plant-eating birds feed on seeds and fruits in the upper branches. Further down, insect-eaters, such as barbets and sicklebills, pick at the insects that pass up and down the trunks. On the ground, doves and tinamous scratch for food in the leaf litter of the forest floor.

▲ THROUGH THE UNDERGROWTH
Cassowaries are flightless birds related to emus that live in the forest of northern Australia and New Guinea. They can run at about 45 kph to escape predators.

◄ MASSIVE BEAK
Great Indian hornbills are plant-eating birds that live high up in the forests of South-east Asia. Their most striking feature is the large horn, or casque, on the bill. This is not as heavy as it looks, since it is hollow. These hornbills feed on fruits such as figs, using the saw-toothed edge of their bills to cut into food. They also eat small frogs and other animals, hopping sideways along branches to get at their food.

CUTTING EDGE ▶
Toucans are not related to the hornbills they resemble but to woodpeckers. They live in South America. This particular toucan feeds on insects, small reptiles and soft fruits.

AMAZING PLUMAGE ▶

The resplendent quetzal is a very colourful bird that lives in the mountain forests of Central America. This small, rare bird flies around the trees looking for fruits and insects to eat. Once it finds a meal, it hovers as it plucks the food from the branch. The quetzal then returns to its perch to eat. Both males and females are brightly feathered, but there are differences. Males have a crest of spiky feathers on their head, and their tail is very long.

◀ SOCIAL CHATTER

The scarlet macaw (left) and the blue and yellow macaw (right), are large and noisy rainforest birds in Central and South America. They feed on hard fruits in the treetops, using their tough bill to crack them open. Macaws are very sociable birds, and they form strong bonds with each other. Some pairs of birds may live together for life.

FIG FEAST ▶

There are no real seasons in a rainforest, as we know them, but less rain falls at some times of the year than at others. In drier times of year there is often less fruit available for birds to eat. Many birds, such as this pale white-eye, rely on figs to see them through the lean times. Fig trees are hardy plants that do well in drier conditions.

Grassland Birds

Tropical grasslands receive much less rain than the forests. Trees need a large amount of water to grow, and few trees can survive in the drier parts of the tropics. Instead of trees, tall grasses grow in the tropics. These tropical grasslands or savannahs include the Serengeti in East Africa and the Matto Grosso in Brazil. Life out in the open is very different from that of the forest. Grassland birds are much less brightly coloured than forest ones. They rely on drab brown and grey plumage to help them stay hidden from predators. For many grassland birds, being able to run fast is just as useful as flying, as there are few high perches around. Ostriches and some other grassland birds cannot fly at all. Instead, they run away at high speed from any danger.

▲ MIGHTY STRUTTER

The kori bustard lives on the savannahs of eastern and southern Africa. At over 1m tall and 20kg, it is one of the largest birds in the world that is capable of flight. However, the kori bustard spends most of its time on the ground. It often runs beside migrating herds of animals and feeds on the insects that are disturbed by the passing herds.

SCRATCHING A LIVING ▶

A flock of helmeted guineafowl gather at a muddy watering hole in Africa. These birds are the tropical relatives of pheasants and other gamebirds, which are more common in the chillier parts of the globe. Guineafowl do not fly well and only take to the air to escape danger. They use their thin toes to scratch around in the ground for seeds to eat.

◀ MEAT-EATERS

A pair of ground hornbills perch above African grassland. These birds are not much like their forest relatives. They are much larger, and they do not have a casque on their bill. Instead, they have a bright red wattle of loose skin on their neck. These birds are chiefly meat-eaters (carnivores). The ground hornbill on the left is holding a chameleon lizard and a large insect in its bill.

▲ IN THE OPEN

This male sandgrouse is incubating eggs in a semi-desert in Namibia. This region is even drier than grassland, and only the toughest plants can survive here. Food is hard to find. Sandgrouse travel around in search of areas that have just been rained on. The rain causes buried seeds to begin to sprout, and the birds are able to feed on these sprouting seeds.

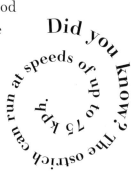

Did you know? The ostrich can run at speeds of up to 75 kph.

▲ GROUP LIVING

A colony of carmine bee-eaters perch outside their communal nest in a sandy cliff. When the breeding season is finished, the bee-eaters will travel long distances looking for food. Despite their name, these birds feed mainly on locusts and other grasshoppers. They catch insects on the wing, using their long, pointed bill.

11

Wetland Birds

While too little water turns a region into a grassland or even a desert, a lot of water will change the habitat as well. Tropical wetlands, such as the Tonle Sap in Cambodia, are havens for bird life. Tropical wetlands are often seasonal, shrinking or vanishing altogether in dry seasons. However, when flooded, they are a good source of food, and many migrating birds travel thousands of miles to feed there.

▲ **SIFT AND SCOOP**
The African spoonbill is named after its oddly shaped beak. This bird spends most of its life in water. It feeds at night and during the day, wading through the shallows, swinging its beak from side to side. The swirls in the water attract small fish, which the spoonbill then scoops up.

▲ **IN HUGE NUMBERS**
Flamingos, such as these lesser flamingos from Africa, feed in huge flocks, which sometimes number more than a quarter of a million birds. They normally live in and around shallow tropical lakes, where the water is very salty or filled with other chemicals that make it inhospitable to other birds. Flamingos wade in these salty lakes and feed on the microscopic plants and animals that grow there.

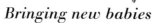

Bringing new babies
European legend has it that newborn babies are brought to families by storks. White storks are migrating birds that arrive in Europe in the spring, when many babies are born. Ancient Europeans believed that the souls of new-born babies dwelled in the marshes and other wetlands where the storks feed, and that the birds carried the souls with them when they came from the wetlands and dropped them down the chimney.

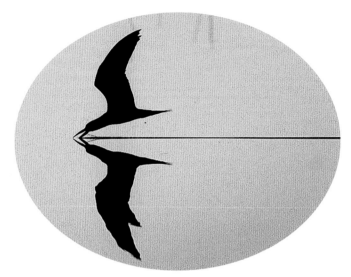

◀ **RED WADERS**

Scarlet ibises are unusual for wetland birds because they have such conspicuous plumage. They nest in trees in large numbers and feed in coastal swamps and mangroves.

▼ **WALK ON WATER**

African jacanas are also known as lily-trotters because they walk on flat lily pads that float on the surface of water. These small birds have extremely long toes that spread their weight over a large area. This prevents the birds from pushing the plants under the water and allows them to pick off insects and other food.

▲ **SKIM AND GLIDE**

African skimmers are related to seabirds that live on coastlines. The lower bill of a skimmer is longer than the upper one. They catch fish by dragging their longer lower bill through the water as they fly above the surface.

ODD-LOOKING BILL ▶

As its name suggests, the shoebill, or whale-headed stork, has a large bill when compared to other water birds. Natives of central Africa, these unusual storks specialize in feeding on fish and frogs at pools that are drying out. They catch their prey as the water level falls.

Sight and Sound

▼ SEEING IN COLOUR

Colour vision is very important for tropical birds that feed on flowers and fruits. When fruits ripen and flowers bloom, they change colour. Here, a sugarbird is preparing to feed on the nectar in the red flowers of an aloe plant.

Birds have excellent hearing and vision because these are the most useful senses that flying birds can have. Although all birds can smell and touch, few rely on these senses. Smelling food while speeding through the air is ineffective. Handling objects with wings and beaks is difficult.

Birds have large eyes compared to their body size, and most have their eyes on the side of the head. Each eye looks at a separate view, so the images are not as clear as those created by human binocular vision. Our eyes look forward and make a detailed three-dimensional view of the same thing.

Birds do not have outer ears. Sound waves get into the inner ear through small holes on either side of the head. These holes are covered by feathers.

▼ SEEING WITH SOUND

South American oilbirds spend the day inside dark caves and cannot rely on their eyes to find their way. Instead they use echolocation (see right) to work out where they are and to allow them to fly in the dark. Each bird makes its own unique clicking sound so that it does not get confused in crowded caves.

HEARING LIKE BATS ▶

Echolocation is an orientation system that uses sound. A few birds that live in caves use echolocation, but nocturnal bats are the true masters of the art. Echolocating animals find their way around by producing loud and high-pitched sounds that bounce off objects as echoes. A near object produces a loud echo that returns quickly, while a more distant object will cause a weaker echo that takes a much longer time to come back.

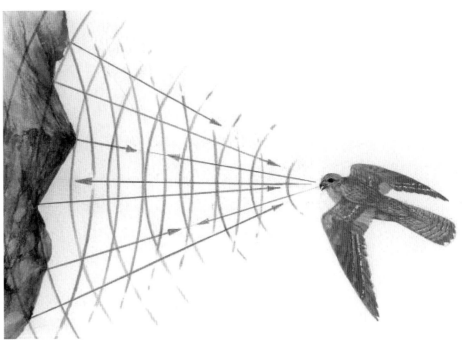

▼ SING A SONG

This black-lored babbler is singing to attract a mate or to defend its territory. Like most songbirds, this Kenyan species belongs to a large group of birds called the passerines. This group also includes sparrows and tits. Passerine songs are produced in the bird's well-developed voice box, called a syrinx. The songs have very complex melodies and are unique to each species. Male passerines sing more often, but the females can sing just as well.

▲ DISH FACE

Like all owls, this great horned owl, which lives in North and South America, hunts in the dark. It uses its large eyes and sensitive ears to locate its prey before swooping in for the kill. The disc of feathers around the face acts like a satellite dish, which channels even the tiniest sounds made by the prey into the ears.

Built for Flight

Birds are the best flyers in the animal kingdom. They do not fly in exactly the same way as aeroplanes or helicopters. The inner section of each wing flaps ups and down, while the outer parts rotate, so that the tips draw a circle in the air. On the downstroke, the long flight feathers are flattened, so they overlap and make a solid surface to push air down and back. This pushes the bird up and forward. After the wing has flapped downward, the flight feathers are twisted to make slits in the wing. During the upstroke air can rush through the wing so it can be raised easily and does not create a drag force that would slow the flight and make the bird lose height.

▲ AGILE FLYERS

Parrots such as these red and blue macaws have long, quite narrow wings that taper towards the tip. These allow parrots to be fast and agile fliers, but also make them able to glide well, when necessary. The position of a macaw's flight feathers, like those of other birds, can be adjusted to change the shape of the bird's wings.

◀ AIR CIRCULATION

Birds need a lot of oxygen to power their bodies when flying, so they have a very efficient lung system. Our lungs suck in air, extract the oxygen and breathe out used air. However, air passes through bird lungs in one direction, so that oxygen can pass continuously into the blood. Air breathed in goes straight into air sacs at the back, and is then pushed through the lungs and into the forward air sacs before being breathed out.

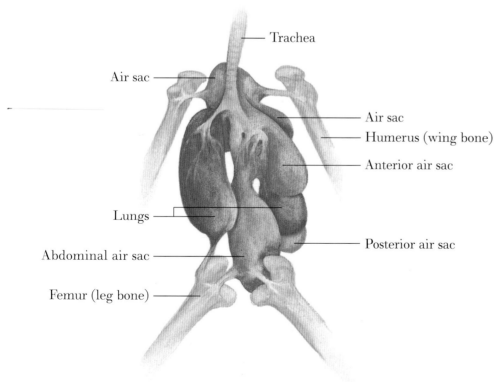

Trachea

Air sac

Air sac

Humerus (wing bone)

Anterior air sac

Lungs

Posterior air sac

Abdominal air sac

Femur (leg bone)

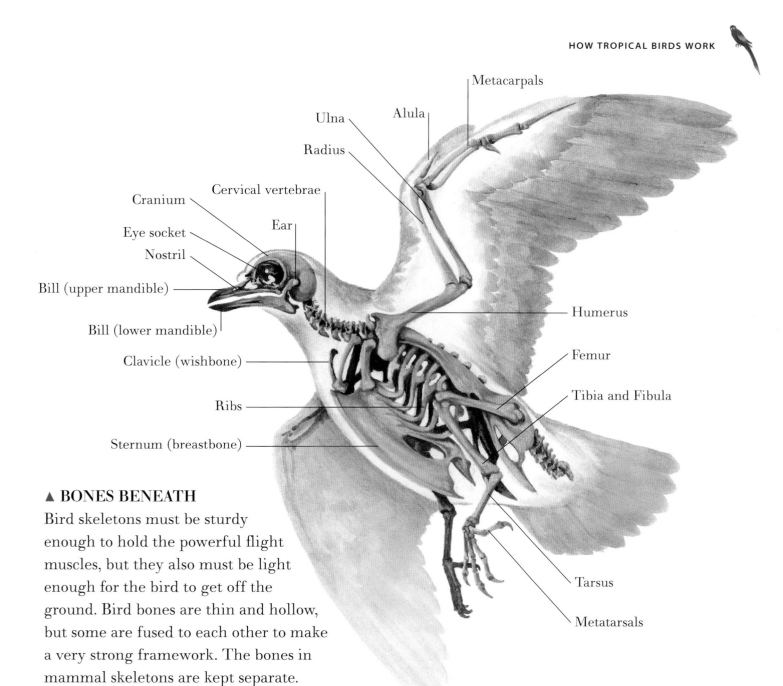

Metacarpals
Alula
Ulna
Radius
Cervical vertebrae
Cranium
Eye socket
Ear
Nostril
Bill (upper mandible)
Bill (lower mandible)
Clavicle (wishbone)
Ribs
Sternum (breastbone)
Humerus
Femur
Tibia and Fibula
Tarsus
Metatarsals

▲ BONES BENEATH

Bird skeletons must be sturdy enough to hold the powerful flight muscles, but they also must be light enough for the bird to get off the ground. Bird bones are thin and hollow, but some are fused to each other to make a very strong framework. The bones in mammal skeletons are kept separate.

DELTA WINGS ▶

This buff-tailed coronet hummingbird has triangular-shaped wings that make it especially good at performing fast and acrobatic manoeuvres in the air when it flies. Hummingbirds can flap their wings so quickly that they can hover in the air as they feed on the sugary nectar in flowers.

How They Fly

Although most birds can fly, they use this ability in different ways, depending on how they live. Some birds fly huge distances while other birds make only short, fast flights. Grassland birds, such as pheasants, do not need to fly long distances because they scratch out their living on the ground. However, they will use their wings to make an escape should they be ambushed by a predator. Different ways of life require very different wing shapes. Many birds of prey, such as eagles and vultures, soar high above the ground for many hours, and they have developed long, broad wings to help them do this. Smaller, faster flying hunters, such as falcons, have sleeker wings that can be folded back to allow the bird to dive at great speeds towards its prey.

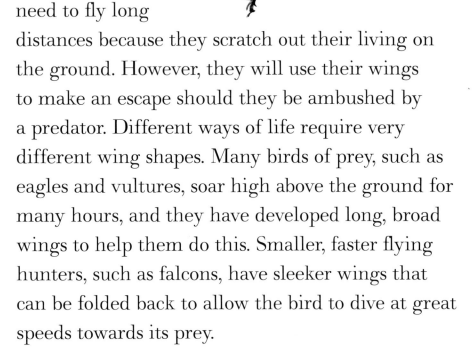

▲ **STRONG MUSCLES**
As this time-lapsed photograph of a Java dove shows, pigeons and other doves are very strong flyers. They have large breast muscles that pull the wings down. The lift force that keeps the bird in the air is generated during the downstroke of each wing-beat. When frightened, pigeons will take off with several noisy wingbeats in an attempt to scare the predator away. This defence behaviour can be very effective indeed.

◀ **SWOOPS AND SWALLOW**
Swallows breed in the cooler regions, but when autumn comes they fly to the tropics. Their long, tapered wings are adapted for making long migration flights. Swallows are insect hunters, snapping up their flying prey out of the sky. Consequently swallows' wings are also thin and pointed enough to be good for the acrobatic twists and turns that they need to perform to catch their prey.

▼ SOARING ON THERMALS

Vultures can spend all day in the air. They use their long and broad wings to catch thermals, streams of hot air that rise up from hot tropical hillsides. The vultures soar effortlessly upward on this rising air and then circle around, looking for food on the ground far below. A flap of their mighty wings prevents them from losing too much height.

FLYING UNDER WATER ▶

Although penguins are more associated with the cold ice floes of Antarctica, one species actually lives in tropical waters. Galapagos penguins live on the islands of that name on the equator in the Pacific Ocean, where they feed on fish like their southern cousins. Like other penguins, this species cannot actually fly through the air, but Galapagos penguins flap their wings to push themselves along under water. They are not really swimming, but flying through the water.

◀ HOVER AND DIVE

A pied kingfisher, a fish-hunting resident of Africa and India, hovers over open water while it prepares to dive under the water to snatch a fish. Kingfishers are one of the few types of bird that can actually hover in the air. Once the pied kingfisher has dived, it floats up to the surface. A single stroke of its small but powerful wings is enough to clear the water and get back into the air.

19

On the Ground

▲ TINY WINGS

A flightless cormorant from the Galapagos Islands spreads its wet wings to help them dry. As you can see, this bird's wings are too small and weak for flight. This diving bird has no predators on land, so it does not need to be able to fly.

Several species of tropical bird have lost all power of flight. The world's heaviest bird, the ostrich, has tiny wings that cannot lift its mighty frame off the ground at all. An adult ostrich weighs 156kg, twice as much as an adult person, and its wings would have to be enormous to lift such a large body. The ostrich and other grassland birds such as the emu and rhea make up for their lack of flying ability with their powerful running legs. The ostrich can reach speeds of 75 kph across the African savannah. Not all flightless birds live out in the open – the cassowary is a large forest bird, and the flightless kiwi lives in the fern forests of New Zealand – but they all find their food on the ground. Kiwis use their long bill to poke about in the soil for worms and insect larvae.

◄ STAND ON ONE FOOT

The flightless kagu lives on the island of New Caledonia in the South Pacific. It is related to cranes and other water birds. It has unique flaps over its nostrils that prevent it from breathing in soil when it digs for food. It spends its days standing almost motionless on one leg looking and listening for insects. The kagu has no defence against newly introduced animals, such as cats and dogs, and it is now threatened with extinction.

▲ GROUND PARROT

The flightless New Zealand kakapo is the heaviest of all parrots. It is most active at dusk, when it waddles across the forest floor, chewing plants and drinking their juices. The kakapo is extinct in the wild and under 100 survive in zoos.

AMERICAN GIANT ▶

The greater rhea is the largest bird in South America, where it roams in large groups across grasslands and deserts. The rhea eats a range of foods, from shoots to worms and lizards. The bird's shaggy feathers provide camouflage among tall grasses. Rheas have a claw at the tip of each of their small wings. The birds use these claws as weapons against predators, such as pumas and other large cats.

Did you know? The flightless kakapo digs out roots with its bill.

WALKING DOWN UNDER ▶

An emu runs through grassland in southern Australia. These birds are the largest in Australia, reaching 1.7m tall. Emus are closely related to cassowaries, which are smaller, also flightless, birds. Emu feathers are not like those of flying birds. Their feathers are more like thick hairs, since they are made up of just a long central shaft. Emus defend themselves from predators by kicking backwards with their three-toed feet.

◀ FLIGHTLESS WANDERERS

Ostriches generally live in large groups, which wander across lowland plains feeding on grass, seeds and small animals. Unusually, these huge birds have feet with two very sturdy toes. With their thick, almost hoof-like claws, these feet are well suited to walking and running over long distances and are powerful defensive weapons.

▲ **UPSIDE-DOWN FEEDERS**

Flamingos, such as this one from the Caribbean, are filter feeders. The flamingo dips its bill upside down into the water and pumps water in and out of its mouth to trap food.

▲ **WIDE MOUTHS**

Tawny frogmouths are insect-eating birds that live in Australia. These birds use their wide mouths to scoop their prey up off the ground and catch insects on the wing.

Foot and Mouth

The bills and feet of tropical birds vary enormously according to how they live. Bills are unique to birds. They are made up of two flexible mandibles, horny extensions that grow from the jaw. Birds of prey have a hooked bill that can rip into flesh, while the bills of other birds are shaped to dig out insects or crack nuts. Most birds have four toes, with three pointing forwards and one backwards. Claws are used for fighting, gripping perches and digging.

BASIC FOOTWORK	
	Scratching: Pheasants and many other ground-living birds have a long middle toe, which they can use as a tool to scratch seeds and other food out of the ground.
	Swimming: Ducks and other swimming birds have webbed feet that are good for propulsion, helping the birds push against water as they paddle on the surface.
	Perching: Perching birds, such as song birds, have a fourth toe that points backwards. This toe wraps around the back of the perch, while the front three grip the front.
	Running: Most running birds have lost at least one toe. Ostriches have lost two, and their claws are thick and short, which helps them run at great speed up to 75 kph.
	Climbing: Birds, such as parrots, that climb well have zygodactyl feet, with two toes pointing back and two forwards. This stops them falling backwards when climbing.

▲ FLEXIBLE FEET

Mousebirds get their name
from their ability to scamper
through flimsy branches, a
little like small rodents. They
live in central Africa and eat
leaves, fruits and buds. They
are so agile thanks to their
unique feet. The two outer
toes are reversible and they
can point forwards or
backwards. Mousebirds can
use their feet to hang upside
down or grasp on to perches.

UPTURNED BILL ▶

This pied avocet is a wading
bird. It has webbed feet
that help it to stand on
lake beds without
sinking. It also has
an unusual upturned
bill. The avocet feeds
by sweeping the tip
through the water from
side to side, and it may
end up with its head under
water as it grabs at its prey.

ALL KINDS OF BEAKS

	Chisel: Woodpeckers have a pointed bill that is used to get food by pecking through bark to get at insects living in wood. Many fruit-eating birds have a similar chisel-like bill.
	Prober: Spiderhunters and many other insect-eating birds have a long curved bill, which they use to probe into crevices in trees and plants to get at their prey.
	Cracker: Parrots have a distinctive, powerful bill, which they use for cracking open the shells of nuts and seeds. The strong jaws crush food between the sharp curved bill.
	Scoop: Skimmers and other birds that scoop up their food, have a longer lower bill. The shape of a bird's bill can tell you a great deal about how the bird gathers its food.
	Sensor: While most birds do not have a well-developed sense of touch, a few use their bill to detect the slightest movements in water. This spoonbill beak does just that.

Focus on

Darwin's finches are a group of songbirds that live on the Galapagos Islands in the tropical Pacific Ocean. They are named after Charles Darwin, the great biologist who visited the islands before publishing his theory of evolution by natural selection in his book, *The Origin of Species*. This theory explains the way an animal or other living thing can change in the way it looks and behaves as it adapts to survive in a new environment. The Darwin finches all evolved from a single species of seed-eating songbird that arrived on the volcanic islands about three million years ago. Today there are 13 species, all of which have evolved to survive in different ways. The most obvious differences are the shape and size of their bills, which have evolved to tackle a wide range of foods.

HOOKED BEAK

The bill of this medium tree finch is more hooked than that of other Darwin finches, and the upper bill is slightly longer than the lower. This means that its bill is better suited for feeding on plant buds when necessary. Tree finches can also eat seeds when they are available, but being able to tackle other food stuffs is useful on the Galapagos Islands, which often suffer from drought.

BLOOD SUCKER

The sharp-beaked ground finch is also known as the vampire finch because it drinks the blood of boobies, a kind of seabird that is common on the Galapagos Islands. It jumps on the larger birds' backs while they sit on their eggs. The ground finch then uses its sharp beak to peck through the boobies' skin, drawing blood which it then laps up. This species is found only on a handful of islands.

Darwin's Finches

CHARLES DARWIN

Although Charles Darwin did not write about the Darwin finches in his book *The Origin of Species*, in the 1830s he returned to Great Britain with several finch specimens following a voyage to the Galapagos Islands. They must have helped him work out his theory of evolution, as did the other wildlife on the Galapagos Islands, such as the giant tortoises, the flightless cormorant and the giant daisy trees.

INSECT-EATER

The rare warbler finch has evolved a longer bill than those of its relatives. Like true warblers around the world, it is an insect-eater. With its longer bill, it has an advantage when it pokes the point into dark crevices and holes in search of creepy-crawlies and other insects.

SMALL SINGER

This small ground finch is thought to be similar to the original ancestral bird. However, some scientists suggest that Galapagos finches might be related to sparrows, or to tanagers, another group of song birds.

SPLIT TONGUE

The cactus finch is a very specialized feeder. Its bill is adapted to feed on the seeds of one particular type of cactus. The bill is longer than in most of the other finches, and the tongue has a pronounced split in it to help the bird feed. Like most Darwin's finches, the females of this species are almost completely black, while the males have brown and grey feathers.

Wings and Feathers

Feathers are made from a protein called keratin, which is also used to make bird claws, mammal hair and reptile scales. Feathers have a very complex structure. The small down feathers preserve body heat. The next layer of contour feathers creates the streamlined shape of a bird's body. The wings and tail are covered in flight feathers. These feathers are much longer and more rigid than the others on the body. Birds use their feathers for more than just flight. The plumage may keep them hidden from predators or it may attract the attention of mates.

▲ **STREAMING BEHIND**

This male standard-winged nightjar has two hugely long streamer feathers that stick out like flags from each wing. This truly remarkable plumage is meant as a signal to females that the male is a good mate. A weaker bird would not be able to cope with the long streamers, which make it harder to fly.

Did you know? Chemicals known as pigments produce the colours in feathers.

◄ **STAYING HIDDEN**

The common potoo's brown and grey plumage helps it to stay hidden as it roosts during the day. It sits motionless on stumps and broken branches and tries to look as much like a piece of wood as possible. It often keeps its large yellow eyes shut to help it blend in.

◄ POISONOUS FEATHERS

Two young hooded pitohuis from New Guinea perch on a branch. They have only just become old enough to leave their nest, and they still have some of the downy feathers that they were born with. These songbirds are unusual because their feathers and skin are naturally poisonous. Like many other poisonous animals, they smell unpleasant. The poison is a defence against predators. If a hawk or a snake eats a bird, it will become sick and quickly learn not to eat another bird with the same coloured plumage.

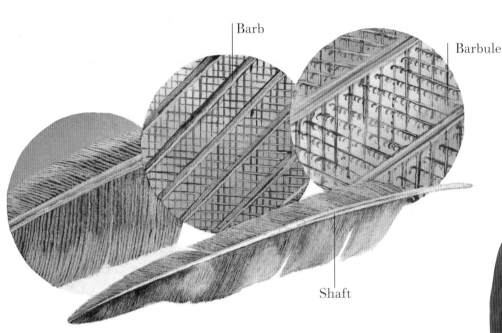

Barb

Barbule

Shaft

▲ A CLOSER LOOK

A feather consists of a central shaft with hundreds of thin branches called barbs. The barbs on the flight feathers are linked to their neighbours by smaller branches called barbules. Tiny hooks on the barbules cling to the barbules of the next barb to form a flat, light surface. When barbs become detached, the bird reshapes them with its beak.

SHOWING OFF ►

This male red cardinal uses his colourful feathers and impressive head crest to make an eye-catching exhibition of himself. Female red cardinals are not red at all. They have olive-grey plumage, which is much better for staying hidden when they sit on their eggs to hatch them. The males use their crest and colourful plumage to attract females. Pairs live together for the spring and summer.

Focus on

Birds of paradise are famous for their spectacular plumage. Residents of the tropical mountain forests of New Guinea, these colourful songbirds do not pair off during the breeding season. Instead, the males compete to attract as many mates as possible. Their bright feathers and skin, and conspicuous tails and crests help the male birds to stand out in the gloom of the forest as they display to the females. Male birds of paradise are generally much brighter and more heavily adorned than the females. Birds of paradise come in many shapes and sizes. The smallest is barely 12cm long, while the longest reaches nearly a metre in length. They may have a short, straight bill or a long, curved one. Most species have rounded wings, which they use to flap short distances. There are 43 species in all, five of which live in the forests of northern Australia.

FEATHER FAN

A male raggiana bird of paradise from New Guinea fans a plume of feathers at a female. The plume feathers grow out of the bird's back, behind the wings. They do not have a rigid shape, but they are held in place by a cross-connecting network of barbs like flight feathers. Some form spirals and streamers.

HERE I AM!

Male birds of paradise make an exhibition of themselves with their brightly coloured feathers, and attract attention by giving loud calls. The plumage of many birds of paradise is iridescent. The light is reflected off the surface of the feathers to create a rainbow-coloured appearance. Iridescence makes the plumage appear all the more spectacular.

Birds of Paradise

LEGLESS ANGELS

Birds of paradise were brought to Europe in 1522 by the survivors of the first round-the-world voyage led by Ferdinand Magellan. Only 18 of the crew got home, but they brought with them several stuffed birds of paradise whose legs had been removed. People thought that since they had no legs they must have flown constantly, like angels, whom they believed had no feet, and so the bird got its name.

TRADITIONAL CLOTHING

The people of New Guinea make elaborate headdresses from the long feathers of birds of paradise to use in their ceremonies. People have been using feathers in this way for thousands of years without affecting bird populations. In recent years, however, much forest has been lost, and many birds of paradise are now struggling to survive.

GATHERING TOGETHER

This male lesser bird of paradise is trying to attract a female. He and several other males have formed a group called a lek, where they can display to females. The female chooses a mate from among the displaying males, and after mating she will go off to rear her family alone. Males mate with as many females as they can manage to attract.

Fruits and Nuts

Many tropical birds specialize in eating fruits, nuts, seeds or nectar. Fruit-eating birds usually live high up in trees, where the fruits are growing. They are most common in the tropics, where fruits are available all year around. Typical fruit-eating birds include parrots, toucans and hornbills. As they eat the fruit, these birds swallow the seeds contained inside. The seed passes through the bird's digestive system and passes out in the droppings. The droppings fall to the ground, where the seed sprouts. Some seeds will not grow unless they have passed through an animal's gut first. Seed-eating birds include finches and pigeons. They peck on the ground, picking out seeds that have already been dispersed and which are preparing to sprout into plants. Eating seeds requires similar mouthparts as eating nuts, because both have hard husks that must be cracked.

▲ FUNKY PIGEON
This spectacular bird is a crowned pigeon, a relative of the town pigeon, or rock dove, that flocks in huge numbers in cities throughout the world. This more colourful relative lives in the rainforest of New Guinea, where it patrols the forest floor feeding on fallen fruits and seeds.

CRACKING NUTS ▶
This blue and yellow macaw is cracking a Brazil nut. Like most large parrots, it holds the nut in its foot and then uses its sharp, hooked bill to crack through the hard shell that surrounds the softer, oil-rich seed inside. Parrots are very strong climbers, and they clamber through the branches to get at their food.

SUGARY DRINK ▶

This white-tipped sicklebill is a type of hummingbird that lives in Central America. The sicklebill does not eat fruits, nuts, or seeds, but drinks nectar, a sugary liquid made by flowers. The hummingbird dips its long curved bill deep into the flower to lap up the nectar. Like most hummingbirds, this sicklebill also snaps up any insects that might be inside the flower too.

Did you know? Nuts generally contain just a single seed, while most fruits contain several seeds.

▲ FRUIT FEEDERS

Silver-cheeked hornbills feed exclusively on fruits. While many fruit-eaters also supplement their diet with insects, these African grassland birds survive by using their strong serrated bill to cut up fruit flesh and crack into nuts. The hornbills feed in trees and hop sideways along branches as they search for food.

SEEKING OUT FRUITS ▶

The crimson-ruffed toucanet has a long, tough bill, which is more pointed than that of its relative, the toucan. The toucanet uses its long bill to reach small fruits in the forest trees of Central and South America. Like larger toucans, toucanets have a sharp serrated bill that is ideal for cutting through tougher foods.

31

SURVIVAL

Insects

Insects are a favourite food of most tropical birds. They are more nutritious than most plant foods and exist in huge numbers. Many insects can be hard to find, being too small to see clearly, buried in soil or chewing their way through wood. Insect-eating birds have many clever ways of getting at their prey. Some birds probe the soil for buried larvae. Agile flyers, such as martins, snatch flying insects out of the air. Most flying insects are available in large numbers for only short times every year, mainly as they swarm together to find mates. Consequently many insect-eating birds have to keep moving throughout the year as they travel to areas with swarming insects.

▲ INSECT HUNTER

As its name suggests, the white-fronted bee-eater mainly eats bees, but it also preys on wasps and other flying insects. This one has caught a butterfly. These birds eat their own weight in food every day. This gives them the energy they need to chase insects through the air.

Did you know? Many insect-eating birds must keep on the move to find their food.

TONGUE IN CHEEK ▶

Woodpeckers use their chisel-shaped bill to find food by drilling through the bark of a tree and into the wood beneath. They are searching for the beetle larvae that eat the wood. Once the woodpeckers have broken through into one of the beetle larvae's tunnels, they can then poke their extraordinarily long tongue into the hole. Sticky barbs at the tip help the tongue grip on to the insects. Once the long tongue is pulled back into the mouth it is coiled up inside the skull.

32

◄ FLUSHING OUT FOOD

A paradise flycatcher parent feeds its chicks by regurgitating insect food from its crop. These birds flush out flying insects such as grasshoppers and moths, which hide on leaves and twigs. They swipe the plants with their wings or fan them with their long tails. Once the insect has broken cover, the flycatcher plucks it from mid-air.

FLEXIBLE NECK ►

This red-breasted wryneck is a relative of woodpeckers and toucans. Wrynecks get their name because they often twist and turn their neck. This behaviour is used as a form of defence, perhaps because the movements resemble those of a snake. This wryneck is collecting termites on a tree trunk. Wrynecks have a long, sticky tongue that is used to lick up food. The birds hunt mainly on tree trunks, but they will also open up anthills to get at prey.

◄ INSECT-EATING PARROT

The kaka is a rare and unusual parrot that lives in the forests of New Zealand. Its bill is less hooked than that of most other parrots. While the majority of parrots feed only on fruits and seeds, this species uses its strong bill to dig into dead wood to expose the insect prey underneath. The kaka also eats nectar.

Focus on

INSECTS AND NECTAR
A broad-tailed hummingbird feeds her young. Nectar is full of sugar and is an excellent source of energy, but it contains few of the nutrients the baby needs. Hummingbird parents, therefore, feed their young mainly on insects. These are full of the nutrients that are needed by the growing young.

The smallest bird in the world is a hummingbird. Bee hummingbirds from Cuba are only 5cm long and weigh just 1.6g. The giant hummingbird from the Andes of South America is 20cm long. Hummingbirds are brightly coloured birds with long bills that they use to sip nectar from flowers. However, these little birds also eat up any insects they come across. Hummingbirds, and the swifts, their less spectacular relatives, have unique wing shapes that make them very agile flyers. They can flap their wings so fast – up to 70 times every second – that they can hover in front of hanging flowers and even fly backwards and upside down. Many people think that hummingbirds never land. They can fly for long periods, mating and even sleeping on the wing, but they do sometimes perch on flowers as they feed.

TRIANGULAR WINGS
A high-speed camera captures the unique wing shape of this male rufous hummingbird as it approaches a flower. The bird's wing is very small. Most of the delta-wing shape is produced by a thin fan of long flight feathers that stick out from the wing tip. The hummingbird's large breast muscles power the wings as it hovers in the air.

Hummingbirds

OLD WORLD COUSINS

Hummingbirds live only in North and South America. In other tropical areas, sunbirds, such as this streaked spiderhunter from South-east Asia, live in a similar way. These birds do not have triangle-shaped wings, and they cannot hover. Instead, they perch on the petals as they dip their long, hooked bill inside the flower. Like hummingbirds, sunbirds eat both nectar and insects, and many also have brightly coloured plumage. However, sunbirds and spiderhunters are songbirds, more closely related to sparrows and warblers than hummingbirds.

FEATHERY TONGUE

A broad-billed hummingbird homes in on a flower as it prepares to lick up the sweet nectar with its feathery-tipped tongue. This species also probes its long bill into holes that have been made by sap-sucking woodpeckers. It licks up any insects that have set up home inside. The length and shape of the bill of each species of hummingbird varies according to the sort of flowers it feeds on.

COURTING CREST

A male black-crested coquette takes off from a branch in a South American cloud forest. This hummingbird is named after the long crest feathers that stick out behind the male's head. While courting, the male flies in a tight semicircle in front of the female, with his crest feathers sticking upwards.

Hunters

Many tropical birds are active hunters with a taste for flesh. Among these are the birds of prey, or raptors, which include eagles and ospreys. These large birds are finely tuned hunting machines. They have superb eyesight, which allows them to scan the ground for prey. Birds of prey have a characteristic tooth-like hook on the tip of their bill. Most also have feet with four heavily clawed toes. They grab and kill prey with these feet and use their bill to rip it up into bite-size pieces. Forest hunters, such as the harpy eagle, find a high perch and sit motionless as they watch for prey to appear. Falcons, that live in more open areas, fly high in the sky before diving at high speed to the ground. It is not just raptors that hunt for food. Some wading birds are formidable fishers, and many smaller birds catch frogs, lizards and mammals.

▲ WIDE WINGS

The Andean condor has the largest wing area of any bird and is the largest bird of prey. This huge bird can soar on the updraughts of warm air that flow up the Andes mountains in South America to altitudes of nearly 6000m.

◄ JOLLY HUNTERS

This laughing kookaburra is devouring a snake. The largest of the birds in the kingfisher family, this bird lives in Australia. Unlike its relatives, the kookaburra hunts on the ground and not in the water. It perches above an open area and swoops down on its prey, which includes frogs, snails and small birds. Kookaburras beat larger prey to death against a stone or branch. The kookaburra gets its name from its manic laughing call.

HUNTING ON FOOT ▶

The secretary bird is the only raptor bird to hunt its prey on the ground. It lives in the semi-deserts and grasslands of Africa, where it hunts for lizards and snakes, and for large insects, such as grasshoppers. The secretary bird flushes out its prey by stamping on tufts of grass. It then gives chase on its long legs and kills animals with blows from its clawed feet.

▼ MONKEY CATCHER

The Philippine eagle is also known as the monkey-eating eagle because one of its favourite meals is the langur monkey, with which it shares the forest. This very rare and impressive bird perches high in the rainforest. When it spots a likely meal, it swoops with remarkable skill through the thick forest branches to grab its victim. Both males and females have a crown of spiky feathers that they can raise around their head.

Did you know? Peregrine falcons reach speeds of 230 kph as they plunge in for the kill?

▲ SILENT FISHER

This great blue heron is gulping down a fish. Since it does not have teeth, it will swallow its meal whole and grind it up into a paste inside its stomach. The heron hunts by sight, standing motionless at the water's edge or in the shallows until its prey comes within striking distance. The heron then extends its long neck and strikes in a flash, piercing its prey's body with its sharp stabbing bill.

Scavengers

Several tropical birds do not hunt for food, but scavenge for leftovers and the remains of other animals' meals. Although it is not a pretty sight, these birds perform a useful function by clearing away dead animals and other mess. The master scavengers are the vultures. These are actually birds of prey, but they leave the killing to others and arrive later to pick the bones clean. Like hunting birds, they have big claws on their feet and the same tooth-like hook on their bill. Several birds that are not scavengers in the wild have adopted this lifestyle after coming into contact with people. Today sacred ibises can often been seen at rubbish tips, using their long bill to root about, picking at discarded meat and any insects they can find there.

▲ TOOL USERS

The Egyptian vulture lives across North Africa and the Middle East. Because of its size, this small vulture is often chased away from food by larger vultures. It therefore scavenges far and wide in its search for food. The Egyptian vulture has also learned to use tools in its search for food. It cracks eggs, even those of ostriches, by dropping stones on them.

SCAVENGING STORK ▶

The Marabou stork is one of the largest land birds in the world, with a wingspan of nearly 3m. While most storks are commonly found in wetland areas, this species is a scavenger and is now a common visitor to rubbish tips. The stork has no feathers on its head and neck, which gives it an ugly appearance, but prevents its feathers from becoming caked in blood as it pokes its head deep into a carcass. This particular individual has a long wattle hanging from its naked neck.

◄ KEEPING CLEAN

This African white-backed vulture appears to have a bald head and neck, but in fact it is covered in fine down feathers. This helps it to keep clean as it feeds deep inside a carcass. These vultures have very long necks, which help them to reach far inside the bodies of dead animals to rip out every last scrap of flesh.

CUNNING COLLECTOR ►

Crows are very intelligent birds and adapt themselves to all sorts of circumstances . This particular species lives across the whole of Africa and Madagascar, where it feeds on all types of food, including carrion – the flesh of dead animals. Like other crows, such as ravens and magpies, this species has learned how to live alongside people.

◄ KEEPING A LOOK OUT

A bearded vulture patrols the skies looking for food. Vultures have excellent sight, and they can scan the ground for dead or dying animals to eat as they circle overhead. Vultures have very wide wings that are ideal for catching the currents of warm air that rise off the ground (thermals). Despite being excellent at soaring, these vultures are not particularly agile fliers.

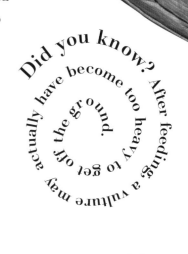

Did you know? After feeding a vulture may actually have become too heavy to get off the ground.

Migration

Many birds, such as storks, swallows and ducks, are winter visitors to the tropics. Since the tropics are warm all year, they are the perfect place for many birds to go when winter begins in the colder regions. Birds take their cue to begin their journey from the length of the day. As winter approaches, the days get shorter, and this causes the birds to set out. A regular journey made by an animal is called a migration. In cooler areas, nature reawakens in spring and summer, and this rapid spurt in growth creates a huge supply of foods for the birds to exploit. Therefore, the migrating birds take to the wing again, leave the tropics and head back to their summer feeding grounds.

▲ GRASSLAND VISITORS
Barn swallows spend summer in northern Europe, Siberia and North America, where they feast on flying insects that swarm during the long, warm summer days. However, as winter approaches and the days shorten, this insect food becomes more scarce, and the swallows head south to the tropics, where insects can be found all year around.

◄ FINDING THE WAY
Scientists are not sure how migrating birds, such as these rainbow lorikeets, find their way when they migrate. It is possible that birds are able to navigate by detecting the Earth's magnetic field with some kind of inbuilt compass. Birds that have never migrated before know in which direction to fly. However, young birds that hatch far away from the traditional nesting grounds end up in the wrong place.

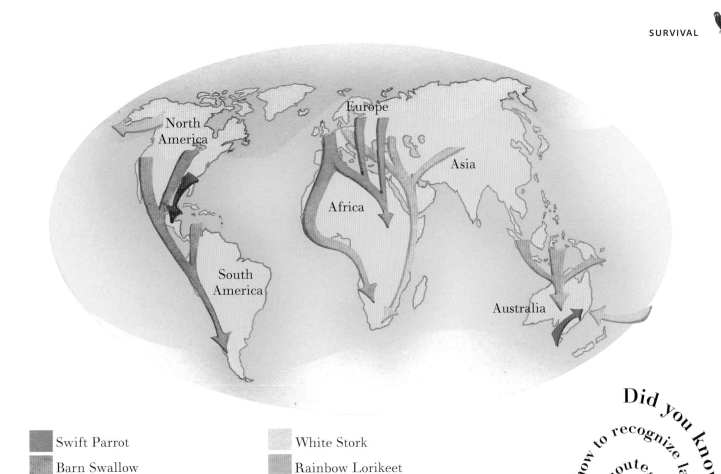

Swift Parrot

Barn Swallow

Ruby-Throated Hummingbird

White Stork

Rainbow Lorikeet

Golden Plover

▲ MIGRATION MAP

As this map shows, migrating birds tend to fly over the land masses of the great continents rather than taking to the open sea. This protects them from the worst storms, and means many more birds complete their journeys safely.

▲ OVER LAND AND SEA

A male American golden plover incubates eggs among the moss of the Alaskan tundra. When the chicks hatch out, they will grow quickly on a diet of insects that are abundant here.

LONG JOURNEY ▶

The ruby-throated hummingbird lives in Canada and the United States in summer and then travels up to 3,220km to the Amazon rainforest in winter. Some fly across the Gulf of Mexico.

41

Focus on

White storks are migrating birds that travel from Europe to southern Asia and Africa every year. They spend the winter months feeding on earthworms, beetle grubs, frogs and small snakes and lizards in grasslands and wetlands in the tropics. They arrive in Europe in the spring. Storks form strong pair bonds and a couple will travel from their tropical wintering grounds to the same nest year after year. Many people build nesting platforms on the roof of their house for them, because a family of storks is thought to bring the household good luck.

COURTSHIP DISPLAY

A pair of storks display to each other during a complicated courtship dance. This includes flapping the wings, bowing the head and snapping and clattering the bill. The storks do this every year as a prelude to mating.

NEST BUILDING

A stork collects grass to construct a large nest during spring. In rural areas, storks nest in large colonies at the tops of tall trees, but they are also a common sight on rooftops in towns.

CLAPPING HELLO

A pair of day-old white storks greet each other in their nest by clapping their bills together. Storks are mute, and they cannot call to each other. Their parents may mate for life.

White Storks

OFF THEY GO

The days get shorter as winter approaches, and the stork colony begins to get restless. This behaviour is caused by a release of hormones that are controlled by light-sensitive glands in the brain. Large groups of storks begin the long migration south at the same time. Scientists do not understand how they all decide to leave at once. The birds stop along the way occasionally, to feed and rest.

SKY SOARERS

Storks are not powerful fliers. They use their wide wings to help them glide for long distances, soaring on thermals and only flapping when they need to gain height. They fly overland, where rising air is more common. Without thermals, most storks are not strong enough to cross wide stretches of sea. They travel via the Straits of Gibraltar into Africa and across the Dardanelles into Asia.

AFRICAN HOLIDAY

These European storks are wading through a shallow lake in Tanzania as more storks arrive at the end of their long migration. During the winter, European storks have very different neighbours than during the summer. Here a herd of wildebeest is wandering past the storks' lake. The storks will stay in the tropics until February or March before they begin the long journey back to Europe. It can take the birds up to two months to complete the trip.

Courtship

Many of the most spectacular features of tropical birds, such as long feathers and bright plumage, are for attracting members of the opposite sex. Tropical birds also often perform complex courtship rituals as they decide whom to mate with. It is generally the male birds that try the hardest to catch the eye of the females. Females have fewer opportunities to breed than males, and they are careful about which males they will mate with. Females produce reproductive cells called ova, or eggs. These contain half the genes needed to make a new individual and all the nutrients it needs for the first part of its development. Males produce reproductive cells called sperm. These contain a half set of genes. One sperm will fertilize one egg to produce a new bird. It is much easier to make sperm than eggs, and males have a much larger number of reproductive cells than the females, so the female birds must choose whom they will mate with.

▲ SONGBIRD

A male western meadowlark sings from a perch to attract females and inform other birds in the area that they are approaching his territory. Male birds that sing the longest and loudest are able to defend the best territories, and good territories make them more attractive to females.

DANCING ARENA ▶

This male whydah or widowbird is so called because its dark plumage makes it look as if it is dressed in mourning clothes. Males clear vegetation to make a dancing ring, or arena, where they can display themselves to females. In the middle of the arena is a tuft of grass that the male dances around, showing off his impressive tail and plumage. If a female enters the ring and shows interest, the male stops leaping around and points his head and tail into the air. After mating, the female leaves the male so that she can raise the young alone.

◄ FANCY THAT!

There is no mistaking a male peacock for a female peahen. The male bird, or peacock, has a huge and gorgeous tail fan with impressive "eyes" at the tip of the feathers and bright blue feathers all over his body. The female peahen is less brightly coloured, and she has no fan. To attract a mate, the male makes an impressive display. He turns to a female, opens his fan, shakes it, and makes a loud, high-pitched call. Successful males mate with a number of females and play no part in raising the young.

◄ MALES ON DISPLAY

This male Andean cock-of-the-rock is displaying at a lek in a mountain forest in Peru. Leks are communal display areas occupied by several males, all jostling for position. The males clear the lek before displaying. This involves spreading the wings and tail feathers and dipping the head. Females passing the lek can choose which male they will mate with.

Did you know? A male cock-of-the-rock's head crest is so large it covers the bill.

SEXUAL BEHAVIOUR ►

This pair of white storks is mating. Unlike mammals, birds have only two openings in their body, the mouth and the cloaca. The cloaca, a word that means "drain" in Latin, passes waste and is also the route by which eggs are laid. During mating, the male passes sperm into the female's cloaca. It travels to the female stork's ovaries where eggs are made.

Focus on

TRUMPET NOISES

Like other cranes, the grey crowned crane has a very long neck. The windpipe amplifies the trumpeting noises the cranes make during their courtship dances.

SPREADING WINGS

The courtship display begins with birds jumping with wings spread. One of the birds performs a ritual flight, flapping its wide wings and leaping toward the other.

Grey crowned cranes are tall wading birds that live in southern and eastern Africa. They feed by stamping their feet on tufts of grass or splashng in shallow water to flush out insect prey. Many crowned cranes travel with herds of mammals to feed on the insects that these large animals disturb on the move. Males and females have a characteristic tuft of golden feathers on their head. Crowned cranes are well known for their elaborate courtship display. This often looks like a dance, since the female mirrors the movements of the male. The dances are a very important method of keeping the bond between the pair strong. Crowned cranes can mate all year round and build their nests in overgrown marshy areas.

Crowned Cranes

FACE OFF

As the dance continues, the grey crowned cranes face each other. One bird displays its plumage and then leaps forward toward the other. The second bird holds its position while opening its wings, and the leaping bird steps backwards to where it started.

BOWING DOWN

As the crane steps back, it lowers its head in a bow. This bow is returned by the partner, and then the dance begins again. The birds may swap roles or the same one may lead the next dance again.

TREE PERCHERS

Crowned cranes are unusual in that they sometimes perch in tall trees, something that other cranes cannot do. Pairs perform dances regularly to reinforce the strong bond between them. The pair stays together as it moves between feeding sites.

Nesting

Birds lay their eggs in nests. The typical bird's nest is a round bowl made from woven plant fibres, but size and location vary widely. Woodpeckers dig out a nest hole in dead tree trunks with their chisel-like bill. Birds of prey build the largest nests, some nearly 2m wide. In contrast, the bee hummingbird makes a tiny cup-shaped nest that is less than 3cm across. Some nests are more elaborate than others. Hummingbirds use the sticky silk from spiders' webs, while many songbirds use mud to hold their nest together. Generally it is the females that do the nest building. Male birds may help females by providing nesting materials, such as twigs, grass and leaves. Once a clutch of eggs has been laid in a nest, the parents must keep them warm until the chicks hatch. Most parents do this by sitting on them. In many species, such as the doves, both sexes take turns to incubate the eggs, but the females generally take on this job alone.

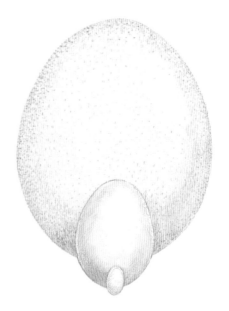

▲ EGGS GREAT AND SMALL
Tropical birds lay eggs in a range of sizes, colours and clutch sizes. Ostrich eggs weigh 1.4kg, while some hummingbirds lay eggs that are less than 0.6g in weight. Grassland birds such as pheasants lay as many as 15 eggs in a clutch. Many eggs are eaten by predators, and only a few hatch successfully.

◄ LIVING TOGETHER
Monk parakeets cooperate to build large communal nests that contain several breeding pairs, such as this one in a palm tree. These parrots live in the open woodlands and grasslands of South America. Nests are permanent fixtures, and birds roost in them even when they are not breeding. New birds that join the colony build their nests alongside existing ones.

▲ MUD CONSTRUCTION

The rufous hornero is an ovenbird. This group
of songbirds is named after the domed nests
they make from mud, which look like large
old-fashioned bread ovens. These long-lasting,
sturdy nests are often renovated by new
breeding pairs or taken over by other species
of bird. Horneros live in open country, and
they feed by probing the ground for insects.

▲ FEMALE PRISONER

This male rhinoceros hornbill from South-east
Asia has cemented his mate and her egg into the
nest inside a hollow tree trunk, using a mixture
of mud and vegetable matter. This keeps them
safe from predators. He will supply food until
the chick is large enough for the female to break
out so that she can help the male find food.

HANGING BASKETS ▶

Crested oropendolas are blackbirds that live in
the forests of South America. They nest together
in large colonies. Each clutch of eggs is laid in
an impressive sac-shaped nest made of dried
grasses, which hangs from tree branches high
out of the reach of many predators.

Fledglings

After growing inside an incubated egg, chicks chip their way out into the world. Most chicks are blind, naked, and unable to stand when they hatch. They are completely dependent on their parents for food. Helpless chicks are called altricial. Hummingbirds, woodpeckers and most perching birds, including song birds, begin life as altricial chicks. A few birds hatch out in a more independent state, known as precocial. Ostriches, ducks, fowl chicks and other mainly ground-living species are precocial. They are able to walk from the nest to feed themselves just a few hours after hatching.

The parents of altricial chicks feed them on insects or juicy fruits. Generally this baby food is regurgitated from the parent's crop, a food sac in the throat. The nutritious food allows the birds to develop and become stronger. The first feathers are fluffy down, and are used to keep the birds warm but are useless for flight. As the birds get stronger, they grow contour and flight feathers and begin to stand on the edge of the nest with their wings outstretched. Young birds fly by instinct, but many take several weeks to learn how to fly properly.

▲ SINGLE MOTHER
Greater flamingos breed in huge colonies, but both parents incubate just a single egg on a mound of mud, and they feed the hatchling on regurgitated plankton.

▼ DEVELOPMENT
A fertile chicken's egg, showing the development of the embryo. The fertilized egg divides to form a ball of cells that gradually develops into an embryo. As the embryo develops, nourished by the yolk sac, the air space at the rounded end of the egg enlarges as water evaporates.

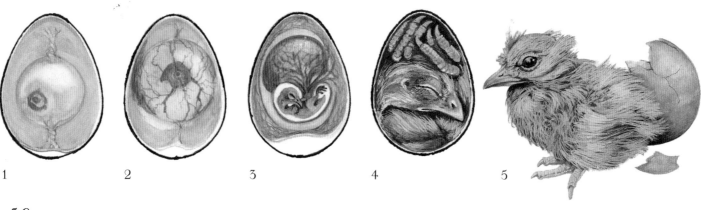

1   2   3   4   5

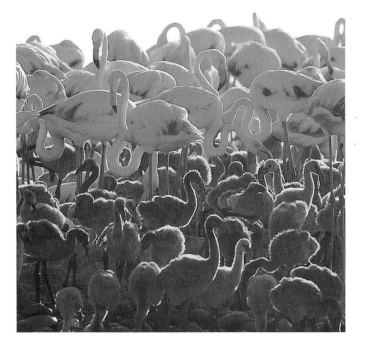

▲ ALL TOGETHER

Once flamingo chicks are old enough, they walk off the nest mounds where they hatched and gather in a crèche. These groups of young are supervised by a few adults, who keep them from becoming lost in the huge crowd of adult birds. Each chick's parents return to the crèche regularly to supply food to their young.

▲ DAD'S IN CHARGE

Unusually, male rheas incubate the eggs and look after the young as they grow. Rhea chicks are precocial. By the time they are a few days old, they can walk unaided and feed themselves. After laying her eggs, the female leaves the nest to search for a new mate.

Did you know? Young birds can take weeks to learn to fly well.

▲ STRANGER IN THE NEST

A young cuckoo is fed by a dunnock, its foster mother. The cuckoo's real mother laid a single egg among the dunnock's own. The cuckoo hatches first, and it then pushes the dunnock's own eggs out of the nest.

COUGH UP, MUM ▶

A female orange-bellied parrot feeds her month-old chick. She regurgitates food into its mouth from her crop. This is a pouch in the throat that birds can use to store food, when there is no more room in the stomach or if they are carrying food back to feed their young. The chick has not yet grown its flight feathers. The fluffy down feathers keep it warm in the nest.

Special Friends

Many tropical birds are closely associated with other animals or plants of a different species. Scientists call this a symbiosis. In some symbiotic relationships, both parties rely on each other for survival. In other relationships, only one party benefits, while the other is not affected at all. Most symbiotic birds live in the second type of relationship. Many insect-eating birds, such as cranes or bustards, follow groups of large mammals, snapping up the insects disturbed by these animals. Southern yellow-billed hornbills forage alongside bands of dwarf mongooses. The mongooses flush out locusts for the hornbills to eat. White-crested hornbills, fairy bluebirds and some drongos do the same thing with monkey troops.

A few birds are parasitic. This means they have a relationship with another species that actually does damage to the other species. Cuckoos are parasitic birds, as are the sharp-beaked ground finches that drink the blood of seabirds on the Galapagos islands.

▲ LEADING THE WAY
A honeyguide perches on a piece of honeycomb. The honeyguide lives in Africa and is so called because it leads animals (and people) to bee hives full of honey. The bird feasts on wax and bee larvae once the hive has been ripped open by its partner, who is usually a ratel or honey badger.

FOOD AND TRANSPORT ▶
Cattle egrets hitch a ride and cadge a meal on the back of a hippopotamus. This species is also known as the "tick bird" because it often rides around on the backs of large mammals, picking at ticks and other skin parasites. The cattle egret also hops down to the ground to feed on insects.

Nature's Fertilizer

Bird droppings make very good fertilizer. They contain many phosphates and nitrates, which are needed by plants to grow. The Pacific coast of South America is very dry – much of it is a desert – and bird droppings deposited in this area by seabirds such as cormorants, boobies and pelicans do not break down in the dry climate. Over the years, the droppings have built up in layers up to 30m deep. People have mined these droppings, known as guano, for more than a century. Today most of this valuable source of fertiliser has been used up.

BIRD'S NEST SOUP ▶

A man collects nests for bird's nest soup from an island cave in southern Thailand. The nests belong to cave swiflets, drab-feathered relatives of hummingbirds, that live in large colonies in the island caves. Like oilbirds, these little birds use echolocation to find their way around in the dark of the cave. Their nests, which are made from dried spit, today are harvested sustainably to make the soup delicacy without harming the swiflet population.

Did you know? Small song birds will eat lice, fleas and other parasites.

CLEANING PARASITES ▶

This oxpecker is feeding on an insect that is living on the impala's hair and skin. Many tropical grassland animals, especially buffalos and antelopes, are infested with lice, ticks and other parasites that feed on their skin, hair or blood. The mammals tolerate being pecked at by these small songbirds because they keep their hides clean of parasites.

Domestic Breeds

Many of the most familiar birds today live on farms, where they are raised for meat and eggs. Chickens, geese and turkeys are related to birds that were originally tropical birds. Scientists believe that all domestic chickens are related to wild jungle fowl that were first tamed and kept for food about 5,000 years ago in India. Over the years, this single species has been artificially bred by people into hundreds of domestic chicken breeds, some of which are raised for their meat while other birds are suited for laying eggs.

Turkeys were first domesticated in Mexico. Other domestic birds include peacocks and peahens, which are tamed relatives of the Indian peafowl. The tamed birds are kept as pets in parks across southern Asia. Peace doves and racing pigeons are domestic breeds of rock doves. These birds are the closest wild relatives of the pigeons that flock in cities across the world.

▲ WILD QUACK

This wild male muscovy duck has much darker plumage than the domestic form. It also has warty red skin around its eyes and nostrils. Like other ducks, this bird has sawtooth-like ridges inside its wide bill to filter out edible particles from water or to grip on to struggling prey. Unlike other ducks it is almost mute.

DOMESTIC DUCK ▶

A female domestic muscovy duck swims with her ducklings. This breed is very similar to the wild form, which lives in South America, except it has white and grey feathers. Other domestic ducks are thought to be related to the mallard. They were first domesticated in South-east Asia and are still kept largely for their meat, although their eggs are also eaten.

COCK A DOODLE DOO ▶

Wild red jungle fowl live in the forests of India and South-east Asia. The male jungle fowl is brightly coloured, with a red wattle on his neck and a skin crest, or comb, on his head. Female jungle fowl are much smaller and drabber. The females make clucking sounds to communicate with their chicks or to warn of danger. The male makes a loud "cock-a-doodle-doo" sound. Wild fowl and domestic chickens are relatives of pheasants and other similar birds that scratch food from the ground.

◀ CHICKEN AND EGG

Despite being bred by farmers for thousands of years, domestic chicken cocks are still more brightly coloured than the hens, just like their wild ancestors. More than 33 billion kg of chicken meat is eaten every year.

LARGER FOWL ▶

The domestic goose is thought to have been bred from the greylag goose, which lives wild across Europe, Siberia and in the tropics in parts of southern Asia. This bird is a waterfowl like a duck , although it has a longer neck, more like another relative, the swan. The long neck helps the goose reach down to the bottom of the water and sift through the mud for food. Geese were originally bred in Europe. They are bigger than ducks and chickens and were once a popular bird for eating at large family gatherings and special occasions, such as Christmas. Today they are thought to be too fatty, and people usually prefer to eat turkey instead.

55

Pets

Birds make popular pets because they do not take up much space and are easy to look after. Many pet birds such as budgerigars and canaries have been bred to have beautifully coloured plumage that is very different from their relatives in the wild. There are thousands of colour varieties of budgie, from the green and yellow of the wild types to completely white or black. Cockatoos and macaws are popular as pets because they can be taught to speak words. Most pet canaries are male because they sing more than the females. Cormorants are popular pets in China, where they may help their owners catch fish. In India and the Middle East, peafowl, with their impressive tail fans, are kept in gardens. Other pet birds include racing pigeons, which can be trained to fly home, even when released hundreds of miles away.

▲ POPULAR PETS
The name budgerigar comes from the Aboriginal word "betcherygah", which means "good food". They travel around in large flocks looking for seeds to eat. Pet budgies are fed dry and soaked seeds and the occasional bit of leaf. Aboriginal people were always pleased when a flock of budgies arrived, not just because they were tasty to eat, but because it often meant that rain was not far away.

◄ FRIENDLY PARROT
Pet macaws are common in South America, where they fly wild, but they are less common in milder regions, where they are expensive and hard to keep properly. Trade in pet parrots is heavily controlled by law and local regulations to prevent people from trapping too many birds in the wild to sell in markets and pet shops as pets. As well as being very intelligent birds, macaws and other large parrots can live for a very long time indeed, sometimes as long as the rest of the owner's life.

Did you know? Male canaries really can sing more than female canaries.

▲ CHATTY COMPANION

It is not just parrots that can be taught to talk. Mynah birds are very good mimics, too. They often copy laughter and whistles, and they can repeat short phrases, although they obviously do not understand the meaning of the phrases they utter. Mynah birds are relatives of starlings, and they originally came from the forests of South-east Asia.

Desert Island Story

Pet parrots are often associated with shipwrecked sailors and pirates. Perhaps they were good company for these men, who spent years without seeing another human being. Robinson Crusoe, a shipwrecked traveller written about by Daniel Defoe, spent more than 25 years on a desert island. For most of his stay, his only companions were a pet parrot and some animals rescued from his ship.

◄ SAVING LIVES

Miners used to take canaries into mines as a simple early warning system of poisons in the air. They would become unconscious a few crucial minutes before the men also became unwell, providing a vital warning of danger for the men who worked far below ground.

Extinction

In the last three centuries, about 80 species of bird have become extinct. Extinction occurs when all of the members of a species die. Many extinctions occur naturally, but increasingly they are caused by the activities of humans, such as hunting and destroying the habitats the birds need to survive. Scientists think that birds evolved from small meat-eating dinosaurs. When the other dinosaurs became extinct 65 million years ago, the ancestors of birds survived. So, in a sense, dinosaurs never disappeared. They are all around us as birds. The first birds probably could not fly as well as they do now. Instead these feathered animals climbed up trees and glided to other perches or on to prey on the ground. Only later did their skeletons and muscles evolve so they could take off from the ground like they do now. Since the first species of bird evolved about 150 million years ago, they have evolved into more than 9,000 species. Most of these birds live in the tropics.

▲ DEAD AS A DODO

Perhaps the most famous extinction was that of the dodo. This flightless bird lived on the Indian Ocean island of Mauritius. When it became extinct in 1680 some species of walnut tree on the island stopped producing new trees. Their seeds needed to be eaten by dodos in order to grow.

◄ MIGHTY MONSTER

The small egg on the right belongs to a chicken, and the huge egg on the left belongs to an elephant bird, an enormous flightless bird that lived on the island of Madagascar until about 900 AD. These 3m-high birds weighed about half a tonne, and each of their eggs held 8 litres of white and yolk. An egg is a single cell, just hugely enlarged, and an elephant bird egg would have been the largest animal cell that ever existed. Elephant birds lived alongside people on the island for about 1,000 years.

Fact or Fiction?

Sinbad the Sailor was a character from the Arabian Nights, *a collection of literature from the Middle East. One of Sinbad the Sailor's many adventures involved being attacked by a giant bird called the roc. This story may be based on the elephant bird of Madagascar. Arab traders often made visits to the island when the birds were still alive. They may have brought back stories of the giant and deadly birds — but to make the story better, they left out the fact that they could not fly.*

▲ GONE FOREVER

The Carolina parakeet is the only parrot species that has become extinct in recorded history. This species was common across the United States until it was last seen in 1904. Most unusually for parrots, this species lived as far north as New York. Hatmakers contributed to the destruction of this species by catching the bird for its orange, yellow and green feathers. The last flock was spotted in the everglade swamps of Florida.

ANCIENT RELATIVE ▶

Archaeopteryx is a famous fossil of an animal that lived more than 150 million years ago. It was the first feathered animal with wings and is generally described as the first bird. Its head was more like a reptile's than a bird's, with a jaw filled with teeth rather than a bill.

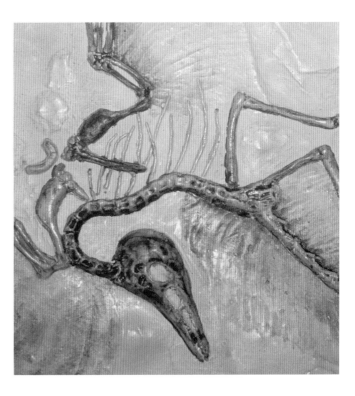

Conservation

Many tropical birds are in danger of extinction. The main reason for this is the destruction of their traditional tropical habitats, especially rainforests, where more species live than anywhere else. Tropical ecosystems are very fragile. Logging companies build roads into rainforests to make it easier to travel through the thick vegetation, and the disruption makes it harder for animals and birds to survive. The introduction of such animals as rats, cats and cattle to isolated communities, including islands, has had a devastating effect on bird life.

▲ **BRIGHT BUT RARE**
This keel-billed toucan is a rare variety of the more common toco toucan. It has a different coloured bill and yellow breast feathers. The keel-billed toucan lives in the forests of southern Mexico, Guatemala and Honduras. A huge area of these forests has been cleared in recent decades, and now these beautiful birds are very rarely seen.

▲ **IN DANGER**
The imperial amazon parrot, or sisserou, lives in areas of thick forest on the island of Dominica in the Caribbean, breeding slowly in the island's mountainous interior. Much of this forest has been cut down during the last century, which has reduced the space needed for such parrots to breed successfully.

▲ **SUCCESS STORY**
Swinhoe's pheasant was once a very rare bird. A resident of the mountain forests of Taiwan, it had been badly affected by hunting and deforestation. However, birds have now been bred in captivity and returned to the wild in protected areas, so the future is looking brighter for this rare fowl.

◄ PUBLIC EDUCATION

This bus, decorated with a picture of the endangered imperial amazon parrot is part of a public education programme in Dominica in the Caribbean to make people more aware of the island's threatened species. Until as recently as the 1990s, Dominicans would hunt these parrots for food. Today the island's people know that they should be proud of their parrots and work to ensure their continued survival into the 21st century.

◄ HOT NEST

The Australian malleefowl builds its own compost heap to keep its eggs warm. As the vegetation rots down, the compost heats up. The malleefowl belongs to a group of birds known as megapodes, which means big feet. In the last 100 years, they have become an endangered species because their habitat has been destroyed and cats and foxes have been introduced into the areas where they live.

HELPING HAND ►

Many of the world's rarest birds have to be bred in captivity to ensure that they survive in the wild. They are kept in large enclosures called aviaries, with enough space for many of the birds to fly around normally. If an area of habitat is protected from development or from hunters, then the birds can be reintroduced to live out their normal lives in the wild. Here a small Puerto Rican parrot chick is being handfed by an aviary worker soon after it has hatched.

GLOSSARY

altricial chick
A chick that is helpless at birth.

binocular vision
Type of vision in which both eyes look to the front and have overlapping fields of view.

breeding season
The time of year when pairs of animals come together to mate and raise a family.

camouflage
Colours, patterns or shapes that allow an animal to blend in with its surroundings in order to hide from predators or escape danger.

carnivore
An animal that eats meat.

carrion
The flesh of dead animals.

cloaca
The rear opening of a bird.

clutch
The set of eggs laid and incubated together.

colony
A large number of birds that gather together to breed.

conservation
Protecting living things and helping them to survive in the future.

courtship
Ritual displays that take place before mating.

crèche
A group of young in the nesting area, which are still dependent on their parents.

crop
A food sac in a bird's throat.

deforestation
Cutting down forests.

down
Fine, hairy feathers for warmth not flight. Young chicks have only down and no flight feathers.

drag
The resistance to movement in water or air.

embryo
The unborn, developing chick.

endangered species
A species that is likely to die out in the near future.

equator
An imaginary line around the middle of the Earth.

evolution
The process by which living things change gradually over many generations.

extinction
The dying out or complete disappearance of a species.

facial disc
A circle of tiny feathers around the face of an owl.

fledging
The time when a bird starts to fly. A fledgling is just beginning to fly.

flightless
Unable to fly.

genus
A group of closely related species.

habitat
The kind of surroundings in which an animal usually lives.

incubate
To sit on eggs to keep them warm so that baby birds will develop inside.

iridescent
Coloured like the rainbow.

juvenile
A young bird, before it grows its adult plumage.

keratin
The essential ingredient of hair, nails and feathers.

lift
The upward force acting on a bird's wings when it moves through the air. It supports the bird's weight.

mammal
An animal with fur or hair and a backbone, that can control its own body temperature. Females feed their young on milk made in mammary glands.

mandible
The upper part or lower part of a bird's bill.

migration
Regular movement from place to place and back again. Many birds fly to warmer climates for the winter.

moulting
The shedding of old and damaged feathers and the growth of new ones, usually once a year.

navigation
Finding the way to a particular place and following a course.

nestling
A young bird is known as a nestling before it has left the nest.

nocturnal
Active by night.

ornithologist
A person who studies birds.

pectorals
The powerful breast muscles of a bird, used in flight.

plumage
The covering of feathers on a bird's body.

precocial chick
A chick that can fend for itself soon after birth.

predator
An animal that hunts and kills other animals for food.

preening
The method by which birds care for their feathers, using the bill and oil from the preen gland.

prey
An animal that is hunted for food.

raptor
Any bird of prey. From the Latin *rapere* meaning to seize, grasp or take by force.

regurgitate
Bring up food that has already been swallowed.

savannah
Region of open grassland found in warm, dry places, such as Africa.

scavenger
An animal that lives mainly on the meat of dead animals.

symbiosis
A partnership between different kinds of animal.

soaring
Gliding high in the air on outstretched wings, riding on air currents.

species
Scientifically, a species is the narrowest grouping of living things.

streamlined
A smooth, slim shape that cuts through the air easily.

thermal
A rising current of warm air, on which birds of prey soar.

tropical
In the tropics, the region of the world close to the equator, where the climate is hot and humid.

tundra
The cold, treeless land in far northern regions of the world, which is covered with snow for much of the year.

wingspan
The distance from one tip to the other of a bird's outstretched wings.

Picture Acknowledgements

l = left, r = right, m = middle
t = top, b = bottom

Corbis: 2br, 14bl, 19bl, 23tl, 25t, 29tl, 31br, 33mr and tl, 34br and tl, 35br and ml, 36tl, 37mr, 39mr, 43ml and tr, 44tl, 46b, 47bl, mr and tl, 51tr, 52br and tl, 53br and ml, 54tl, 56bl and tr, 57bl, tl and tr, 60tr and bl, 61br, ml and tl, 64tr and bl/Theo Allofs: 3br, 16tr, 62tr/ Martin Harvey: 12ml/Peter Johnson: 9br, 11ml. Ecoscene: 3tr, 8tl, 9ml, 10tl, 11br, 17br, 19tl, 23tr, 25mr, 26tr, 29tr, 30tl, 37tr, 38tl, 50tr, 53tr, 55br, 59br. NHPA: /A.N.T.: 6tl, 20br, 33bl/Daryl Balfour: 4bl, 5br/Bruce Beehler: 27tl, 28br and tl/G.I. Bernard: 30br, 49br, 58tl, 59tr/ Joe Blossom: 7bl, 42br, 54br/John Buckingham: 40bl, 51bl/Bill Coster: 21mr, 24bl, 45ml/Stephen Dalton: 4tr, 18bl and tr, 63tr/Manfred Danegger: 42ml and tl, 45br/Nigel J Dennis: 12tr, 13ml, 32tl, 38br, 39tl, 60br/Melvin Grey: 11tl/Ken Griffiths: 6bl, 36bl/Martin Harvey: 5tr, 8ml, 10br, 20tl, 21bl, 62bl/ Brian Hawkes: 14br/Daniel Heuclin: 20bl, 37bl, 58bl/Hellio and Van Ingen: 51tl/E.A. Janes: 55tr/Ralph and Daphne Keller: 22bl/Stephen Krasemann: 40tr, 41br/Mike Lane: 22tl, 55ml/David Middleton: 15ml, 24tl, 25br and ml/Haroldo Palo Jr: 48bl/Peter Pickford: 13mr/Christopher Ratler: 43br/Andy Rouse: 21tr/Kevin Schafer: 9tr, 26tl, 31tr/J and A Scott: 31ml, 44br/John Shaw: 13br/Morten Strange: 15br, 35tr, 49tl/Karl Switak: 29bl/ James Warwick: 49tr/Dave Watts: 7mr, 51br/Martin Wendler: 5ml/Alan Williams: 7tl, 41ml, 45tl/Norbert Wu: 19mr/Daniel Zupanc: 6mr.

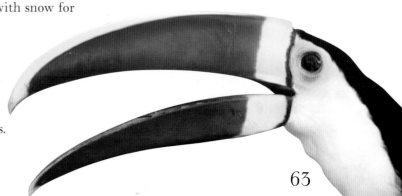

INDEX